Hidden in the Soil

Written by Abbie Rushton

Collins

This person looks for things hidden in the soil.

a pot

Look! It is a coin.

It has been in the soil for years and years.

Wow! This is a big jar.

It was for food or oil.

This wooden ship was deep in the mud.

Look at it now!

This chair was dug up too.
It was for a king.

earrings for a king

Things might be hidden
in the soil near you!

Look at the hidden things

🐾 Review: After reading 🐾

Use your assessment from hearing the children read to choose any GPCs, words or tricky words that need additional practice.

Read 1: Decoding

- Ask the children to read page 12. Ask: What does **might** mean? (*could*) Ask: What else can the word "might" mean? Prompt with phrases, such as: "The dog tugged at the lead with all its might", "She pushed at the locked door with all her might".
- On pages 4 and 5, ask the children to find words with /oi/ or /ear/ sounds, and to point to the graphemes. (*coin*, *soil*, "oi"; *years*, "ear") Repeat for /ear/ on page 11. (*earrings*, "ear")
- Model reading page 10, slowly but fluently. Challenge the children to read page 12 in a similar way. Say: Can you blend in your head silently when you read these words?

Read 2: Prosody

- Focus on the use of emphasis to show feeling and emphasise meaning.
  - On page 6, encourage the children to read **Wow!** with emphasis and in an excited tone.
  - Ask: Which word in the next sentence explains why the person is excited? (*big*) Encourage the children to read the whole page, emphasising **big** in the second sentence, too.
  - On page 7, discuss which word to emphasise (e.g. *by emphasising "or", the reader makes it clear that the jar might have held one of two possible things*).

Read 3: Comprehension

- Ask the children to describe anything they have seen that was dug up, such as in museums, in books or on television. Prompt with examples, such as treasure or dinosaur bones.
- Discuss what we learn about people's lives when we find hidden things. Return to pages 10–11 and ask: What sort of life do you think this king had? What else might he have worn?
- Turn to pages 14–15. Ask the children to describe their favourite hidden thing. Ask: Would you be excited to find this? Why?